CONTAINER GARDENING

Copyright © 2019 Eric Jason

All Rights Reserved. No portion of this book may be reproduced or used in any manner whatsoever without the expressed written permission of the author.

TABLE OF CONTENTS

INTRODUCTION 5

CHAPTER ONE 8

Why Grow Plants In Containers? 8

CHAPTER TWO 21

Designing for Containers 21

CHAPTER THREE 33

Choosing the Right Pot Size for Every Plant 33

CHAPTER FOUR 45

Best Plants for Every Pot 45

CHAPTER FIVE 62

Growing Edibles 62

CHAPTER SIX 69

Companion Planting 69

CHAPTER SEVEN **75**

Plants for Year-Round Container 75

CHAPTER EIGHT **82**

Maintenance Tips for Healthy Containers 82

CHAPTER NINE **87**

Vertical Gardening 87

CHAPTER TEN **94**

Managing Pests and Plant Diseases 94

CHAPTER ELEVEN **99**

Harvesting and Storing the Bounty 99

CONCLUSION **102**

INTRODUCTION

Container gardening practice allows you to garden all year round irrespective of your outdoor climate. Plants grown in containers are more accessible, give little chance to weeds, and require the use of fewer gardening tools. You can rearrange them in a way that suits your taste and needs.

Growing plants in pots allow for mobility, especially when you need to get them exposed to the sun. You can quickly move them outside for exposure to sunlight, and they can be moved inside for adequate protection when it gets windy or cold outdoor.

When containers are being placed on the balcony or deck of your house, they add value and beauty to such area and also make fresh vegetables available to the family. A container gardening project is also an excellent way to start gardening because it can be done with little effort on a small scale.

What is Container gardening

Container gardening can be referred to as the growing of plants such as fruits, herbs, and vegetables in containers. It is an ideal practice for people living in high-rise apartments who do not have access to outside spaces. This system of gardening also works fine for people with a limited budget that can't afford to maintain a regular garden.

Container gardening can be used in creating a stylish simple garden space using high or low maintenance, depending on what works for you. It is ideal for people who find it difficult to bend down due to old age or any other health challenges. Setting large containers of 2 or 3 feet high, on the ground makes it easier for you to reach and makes the plants less prone to weeds, unlike conventional gardens. With this system of gardening, you can create an attractive planting design quickly, which will, in turn, become a center attraction.

CHAPTER ONE

Why Grow Plants In Containers?

Container gardening is an alternative to regular gardening in so many ways. Most people are attracted to this practice by growing ornamentals or edibles while targeting a practical outcome based on their efforts. Some engage in it for appealing, flourishing plants it tends to provide. Irrespective of the reasons, gardening in container promotes you beyond space and time constraints while allowing you to enjoy this creative style of gardening all year-round. The following are among the reasons for growing plants in pots:

Gardening at Your Convenient Time

The urge for gardening depends on the weather most times, where a good number of gardeners prefer to garden at the beginning of the planting seasons. The time of growing your plants usually depends on your geographical location. Considering the temperate regions, for example, you will have to garden as the winter approaches and the frozen ground wipes off the surface of the earth. While when it comes to the tropics, planting is executed at the starting of the rainy season.

Fortunately, when you choose to grow plants in a container, there is no need to wait for the weather or any other external factors before you begin growing plants. So this allows you to garden all year-round.

It is an Easy Gardening Method for Beginners

In traditional gardening, some specific factors will typically occur, for example, weeds that have seeds that grow faster than the very plants' seeds we intend to grow. That is the reason why most of the experienced gardeners dedicate more energy and time to prepare their vegetable bed. If you plant your garden with less preparation, you will be at the risk of having your beds overrun with weeds in no time. And this can be quite discouraging, especially to the beginners.

Other factors that may spring up includes pest and diseases that also affect outdoor gardening. Fortunately, container gardening comes with little weed problems. You can also control the menace of pests and diseases quickly due to their small size. Easy mobility of containers also allows you to move them to more sheltered spots when there is a risk of prolonged odd weather.

Elimination of Space Constraints

People living in high rise apartments or townhouses are usually faced with space constraint issues, especially when it comes to in-ground gardening. Because they mostly don't have outdoor spaces to call their own. Fortunately, if it is pot gardening, all these shouldn't be a problem.

You will never be restricted to gardening due to space. The container makes it easier to have several plants growing up in your window sill, balcony, or any bright spot with adequate exposure to sunlight. Gardening in pots also allows you to have varieties of plant grown in the same container, by using companion planting style. And this helps in producing higher crops and making farming a possibility for all and sundry.

Bringing Gardening Indoors

Container gardening allows you to grow hundreds of houseplants that will conveniently grow indoors, especially when planted close to a sunny window. Fruits and vegetables can be grown under the right conditions when they are being exposed to sufficient sunlight, and even in the absence of the sun. Artificial lighting can also be used.

Another example is the growing of flowering and compact leaf using warm lights coming from the orange-red spectrum that works well for growing capsicums and tomatoes. Vegetables can also be grown under hi-tech lighting arrangements that can be tweaked easily periodically to suit specific developmental stages. And this will, in turn, help in producing maximum yield for a given space.

A lesser Amount of Water is Required

Container gardening requires less water when compared to traditional gardening. In regular gardening, when you provide enough water to the plants, the water will end up spreading to the surrounding soil. And water will evaporate quickly due to the larger surface area of the land, causing it to dry off quickly, thus call for more watering.

On the other hand, plants in containers such as tubs and pots will demand less water because the loss of water via evaporation will reduce due to the decreased surface area. And the loss of water is only restricted to the top layer of the soil. The only disadvantage here is that potted plants alway get limited access to water. Unlike the regular gardening that roots can grow deeper into the ground and derive water from the lower layers of the soil. Therefore container gardening needs careful checking of the dampness of the dirt, and this can be quickly done by dipping your finger into the soil.

No need of tilling

Tilling the ground can be quite hard and back-breaking. It has also been discovered that by tilling the soil, many natural organisms that are needed for a healthy garden ends up being disturbed. And this is why most gardeners are switching to a no-till garden option. That is where container gardening becomes necessary, as you are allowed to create a conducive gardening environment. You can incorporate healthy components without having to amend the soil, or be worried about the damage that might be caused by tilling.

Easier Pest Management

The control of pests in containers' plants is much easier because in this case, a chemical application may not be required. You can even get to handpick more giant insects and make use of cotton bud to dip-in rubbing alcohol to get rid of scale insects or aphids.

The individual pot can also be dunked into lukewarm water to help in drowning all unwanted soil organisms. Keeping the container in a plate that is filled with water can also help in preventing ants from entering your pot.

Fertilizers Management

Container gardening plants require less application of fertilizer. Similarly to watering, when fertilizers whether organic or chemicals are applied to potted plants, they do last longer. The reason for this is that they remain concentrated within a limited amount of soil available in the container.

Another great advantage is that pot will not get to share fertilizers with competing weeds. And this is why they should be sparingly in containers to avoid high concentration of the fertilizers from burning the roots. Make sure you select high-quality organic fertilizer and restrict yourself to the use of your compost.

Easy Adjustment of Growing Conditions

Container gardening makes it easier to use container plants without the need to undertake amendments of large-scale soil. A slightly acidic medium can be provided for your blueberries and rhododendrons without affecting the pH of the soil inside the other containers and even garden beds.

In a situation where there are seasonal differences in terms of the light intensity, the plants can be rearranged accordingly. Once the plants have similar watering needs, they can live in harmony as long as they are housed in different containers.

Easy adjustment of the garden height

If your movement is restricted due to some physical limitations or you don't want to bend down to tend to plants, container gardening will work for you.

You can have your pots or tubes arranged at a convenient height or ledge so that they are easily accessible. It makes feeding, watering, and even deadheading much easier. You can also maximize space usage by keeping the plants arranged at different heights.

Selection of the Growing Medium

Gardening with containers allows for experimentation with the use of different growing media and techniques. An example of this is growing your vegetables in an inert media such as the expanded clay pellets which are intermittently bathed with a nutrient solution. Using this technique helps to increase production and protect your plants from diseases that are caused by pathogenic bacteria and fungi, which are common to garden soil. Sphagnum and coco peat are also alternatives that can be used.

An easy change in garden design

Another advantage of container gardening is the ability to change the look and the theme of your garden by changing the containers. For instance, using large stone containers that have different architectural shapes can provide your patio with a classic look. Making use of acrylic containers as well as a monochromatic scheme in your garden is a way of making it beautiful and as elegant as you want.

Harvesting Made Easy

Harvesting of your vegetables and fruit are easier when grown in containers. Blueberries and strawberries can be grown in pots. Root tubers such as radishes, carrots, and sweet potatoes are also great. And once they are ready for harvest, instead of having to dig them up, you can have the pots overturned on a plastic sheet to avoid crops damage.

.

CHAPTER TWO

Designing for Containers

Few containers can be arranged in all directions but with some proper planning. A well-planned container garden can effectively compete with any garden landscape. The use of different matching pots arrangements, including plantings that vary in height and scale can help in unifying steps, pedestals, railings, and landings.

Ensure growing your plants in a series of matching containers that are systematically arranged to get a formal look. While in the case of a casual garden, the annuals, mix shrubs, and perennials, can be arranged in different containers.

Getting containers hanged on an overhead beam or having them attached to walls helps in beautifying any space they are placed. However, it's imperative to anchor them securely, especially in a situation where they are placed over walkways or on railings.

A timely visit to your garden to catch fun is another factor that should be considered when designing your garden. In a situation where you usually get to visit your garden in the late afternoons or early evening, you can grow plants that exhibit fragrances at night. Plants that are made up of white flowers would also shine at nighttime.

By repeating your growing, the plants themselves, the shape or leaf color produces a unifying effect. And also adding plant or container that stands out when compared to other colors, height or size in such a brilliant way to help provide a focal point.

Selecting the Right Containers for Plants

Containers are designed in different shapes and sizes such as round, square, flat planters, cylinders, or even pots that are adorned with decorative edges. Also, there are specialized pots such as the strawberry pot that can accommodate plant selections with strawberries.

When selecting containers for gardening, always look out for the ones that will accommodate the final size of plantings. And always be prepared to transplant when plants have germinated. Make sure you keep enough space for the plant's roots and always check if they grow down or out.

The positioning of Your Container Gardens

If you have high rise apartments with balcony and rooftops, container gardening is the ideal practice for such locations as they add color and beauty to the area. Nevertheless, some factors should be kept in mind when planning for these spaces. The most important considerations are the weight and drainage system, taking pot as an example; they are heavier when filled with potting mix and plants. Therefore you will need to check the load-bearing capacity that your structure possesses in a situation where you intend using anything other than smaller pots.

Weather Consideration for your Containers

In designing your garden, you need to take weather conditions into proper consideration and determine if the intended space is ideal for the placement of your garden containers. An example is having your pots on the rooftop. It might result in its exposure to intense heat. And when placed in balconies, there may be increased sunlight and heat reflection from the walls. As a result of this, some components might be needed to help prevent overexposure of sunburn.

When it comes to the rooftop and balconies, wind direction is an essential factor to be considered. Because it might end up blowing away your plants or even the containers, that is why you will need to have your plants protected. In this case, you can protect them with panels or by adding screens, anchor your containers can also be of help.

On the other hand, balconies might be obstructed by site orientation or overhead structures from allowing enough sun to get to the plants. When this happens, it is advisable to go for plants that only require lower heat levels.

Selecting Materials for your Containers

Choosing the right container is the first step to a flourishing container gardening. It is essential to used materials with a good match with the plants you are planning to grow in terms of style and size. It should also have a perfect match with your house and the landscape.

The thumb rule can be employed in deciding the right color scheme of one to three colors, after which you can choose containers within the color range. By considering all these, irrespective of the plant that is purchased, the pots will also blend.

There are different kinds of containers that can be used for gardening, such as the traditional terra-cotta pots. There are also containers made of plastic, metal, and wood. Note that anything that can hold soil, water, and allow for natural drainage is ideal to be used for planting. Nevertheless, avoid using dark containers as they can retain heat that might in turn cause overheating to the plants.

Terra-cotta and Stone Containers

The terracotta and stone pots have been used for centuries and are known to blend well with most garden styles. These containers are also porous, thus helps in preventing soil from becoming excessively soggy and protect the plants' roots from drowning. Terra-cotta is designed in different styles ranging from plain to elaborate; there is also a tiny and bigger size.

The problem of these types of containers is their weight though it is an advantage when there is heavy wind. As they will remain stable no matter what and it will be difficult for the plants to be moved. It is essential to water these containers frequently since they are porous. And it is to be noted that minerals and salts will leach out of the soil, causing white stains on them. The spots can be easily cleaned, so it is nothing to worry about. Another downside is the effect of snow or frost, which can cause them to damage or break easily.

Plastic Containers

The plastic containers are non-porous and will retain water. It is ideal for dry climates. They can be moved around easily due to their lightweight. The high plastic containers are an excellent choice for rooftops and balconies because they can withstand any weather conditions. New plastic containers have been endowed to be self-watering.

The disadvantages of these containers are the issue of insulation, water retention, and weight. In wet climate regions, you must ensure that the plants have access to adequate drainage. Also, remember that you will need to anchor the plastic containers during the windy condition and the low quality plastics may crack after a few years due to sun exposure.

Wood Containers

The wooden containers are usually in rectangular or square shapes, which are ideal for formal or contemporary gardens and other garden styles. When containers are made with wood that resist rotten, they will last much longer and wiil not crack even in extreme weather. To add to their durability, they are designed with at least an inch thick on the sides, thereby keeping the temperature of the soil moderate even at extreme outdoor temperatures. However, it's important to note that untreated wooden containers are porous, and when sealed, wood can hold water. Hence the need to guarantee correct drainage system.

Metal and Concrete Containers

Metal containers are known for holding water, which is ideal for dry climates, but not suitable for wet environments. They also do not insulate well and can get tarnished.

Nevertheless, concrete is becoming more popular in the gardening world because they are more porous than metal containers. They are very durable, but the larger they are, the more they become heavy. In general, it is essential to note that concrete pot is not a perfect choice for every garden style.

Ceramic Containers

The ceramic containers share the same characteristics with the terra cotta containers, though they are more expensive. They will last much longer and add beauty to any garden in which they are used.

Other Container Types

Apart from the wood, plastic, terracotta, which are the most popular container choices, anything that can hold your potting mix, and plants can be used for farming. Container gardening requires some creativity. You can use old wheelbarrows, drainage pipes, baskets, wine barrels, wagons, and chimney pots. As long as they can hold your potting mix and plants successfully.

CHAPTER THREE

Choosing the Right Pot Size for Every Plant

To set up a magnificent and reliable potted garden, you need to start up with the right container, especially putting the container size into consideration. When large plants are grown in a small pot, they tend to dry out quickly, causing them to stick to the pot. Conversely, growing small plants in large pots can make the regulation of the moisture in the soil quite tricky.

Importance of Container Size

In as much as you are trying to get a container that is big enough for your plants, you should also put the plant size into consideration. That is because if the plant grown in a pot is too small, its growth will be stunted while its roots become pot-bound, causing the soil to dry out quickly.

Also, when small plants are grown in larger containers, they will be thrown off balance, because the plant roots can't reach the bottom of the pot. With obstruction in the drainage hole, there will be an accumulation of moisture content at the bottom of the container, leading to a mass of soggy soil. When this happens, you will be faced with the problem of root rot and an extra-heavy container as well as a funky wet-soil smell.

Selecting the Right Size of Container

Ornamental Plants

The type of plant you intend to grow, including the depths of the roots, determines the amount of soil that will be needed and the size of the container you will use. Therefore, when starting gardening, ensure you keep the quantity of the soil proportional to the type of plant, including its size to help with the balance soil moisture. Taking note of the following will help your selection:

- Annuals will need a soil depth of 12 inches
- Shrubs will need a soil depth of 18 inches - 2 feet
- Small trees will need a soil depth of 2 - 3 feet.
- Small succulents will need shallow soil which is less than 6 inches.
- Perennials will need a soil depth of 12 - 18 inches

Edible Plants

You are advised to give more room to plants grown as crops in containers. When growing your edibles, it is crucial to put the following into consideration:

- When growing shallow-rooting crops such as strawberries, radishes, and lettuces, you can grow them successfully in 6 to 12 inches soil depth.
- For the citrus and other fruit trees, a soil of about 2 to 3 feet deep will be needed.
- Large scale edible plants such as potatoes, tomatoes and the full-size berry shrubs will require at least 18 inches or about 2 feet soil depth.

- The medium size edibles such as eggplants, peppers, squashes, corns, and melons will need a soil depth of at least 12 to 18 inches.
- Herbs grown indoors will require a soil depth of 6 inches while the ones grown outdoors, will require a soil depth of 12 inches.

Container Shapes

Apart from the size, container shape is also an essential factor that affects the growth of plants. When choosing a container design, it is vital to keep both shapes and sizes into consideration.

Square, Round, and Rectangular

Medium or large size containers with square or rectangular shape, with a depth of about twelve inches to three feet, are perfect choice fo small trees, shrubs, and flowering perennials. If you intend to combine multiple crops, you are advised to make use of larger containers to create enough space for each plant to grow.

Tall and Upright

If you use tall and skinny containers, it will help in elevating small plants and in adding more visual impact. However, it's imperative to be careful when growing a shallow-root plants such as a succulent with a large pot filled with dirt. As it can be easily over-watered and have wet soil collected at the base of the pot beyond the plant roots.

Vase-shaped

When growing combinations of flowering perennials, annuals or small trees, containers that do flare out at the top are excellent options. The reason is that their wide opening creates a lot of space to put together a plant combination. It is therefore imperative to select the container depth based on the types of plant you are including.

Shallow

If you are cultivating small succulents like stonecrop, a low bowl with less than six inches of soil depth can be used. And you can use a plant stand to help raise flat containers a bit nearer to the level of eye. Shallow pots also work perfectly when used as toppers for outside dining tables and side tables.

Urn-shaped

The classical style urn, which is wide at the bottom but having a tight neck and broader opening, is ideal for annuals and perennials that can be easily removed. However, this shape is not suitable for deep-rooted plants because once the root ball forms below the neck of the urn, it will become tough to remove the plant.

Making the Right Match of Container for your Plant

Since the size and shape of containers affect the growth of plants in it, you will want to select vessels and plants at the same time. When selecting a container based on plants, you don't need to rely on the initial size of the plant. You should look out for the plant's mature sizes that are often displayed on the back of the plant label. And also check out for the plants' category if it is annual, succulent, perennial, tree or shrub.

Also, ensure you choose a container that gives enough room for the plants' growth and the soil depth that will provide ample space for roots to spout.

Important Considerations for Growing Edibles

If crops such as peppers, tomatoes, eggplants, and zucchini are grown in full containers, they tend to compete for nutrients, and this can eventually lead to small production.

For this reason, it is advisable to provide each large and medium size edible plant its own pot. And you can as well have pollinator-friendly plants such as the marigolds or herbs tucked around the base if there is excess space.

Containers used in growing edibles are big feeders that enable them to hold lots of soil nutrients which in turn facilitate their growth.

Re-potting your Plants in a Container Garden

When plants are left for a long time in containers, especially when they have outgrown such containers, they become uncomfortable. To know when your plant needs to be re-potted, you will want to look out for these signs:

- Plants will become overgrown and will no longer be proportional to the pot they are being grown.
- When they are watered, the water will run out of the pot, quickly indicating that the roots are taking up most of the space instead of soil absorbing the water.
- You will begin to discover the yellowing of the leaves, stunted growth or plants starting to dry off.

How to Re-potted your Plants

To get your plant repotted, you are required to take the following steps:

- Select a container that is at least a few inches larger in terms of the depth and width than the original container.
- Make sure you dig about four inches or more deep to loosen the roots when removing the plants. After which you can then tug the plant free carefully using a hand trowel. Ensure keeping the root ball intact as much as possible.
- Fill the new pot with fresh potting soil and immediately carry out the process of transplanting.
- Make sure you water well and soak the potting soil.

CHAPTER FOUR

Best Plants for Every Pot

Every season is an opportunity to grow a particular crop. Therefore gardeners always have the desire to get crops planted in both the summer and springtime. There are varieties of vegetables and fruits that can be grown in containers. These include tomatoes, cucumbers, bananas, and many more.

They can be grown on your porch, decks, and wherever you want to grow them within your space, and they will thrive in containers. So you don't have to worry about not growing them traditionally. Whether you have an ample gardening space or not, if you want to have your foods grown yourself, containers would be of great help.

Basil

Basil can be grown indoors or outdoors, it is very delightful in soups and other recipes. You can cultivate this plant and use it for your favorite dishes when the need arises. All you need for this is some organic potting soil, a six-inch planter including the basil itself.

Note, when watering basil, avoid getting the leaves and stem wet. Preferably, pour the water directly onto the soil. Remember to always get the herb exposed to a bit of sunlight every day, especially when they are grown indoors. You can also plant basil in pots that can be moved quickly towards the deck when the sun is at its peak during the day.

Strawberries

Though strawberries need ample space to thrive, they will still grow well in containers even when grown indoors. This fruit needs adequate access to sunlight. Therefore, you can place them in sunny areas, preferably close to the window. In the winter season, when there is less sunlight, you can use artificial sunlight which keeps them available for all-year-round growth. Grow them in pots large enough to handle the number of their crops and then harvest them regularly to give space for more growth.

Tomatoes

Tomatoes also do well when grown in containers. They can be grown in any sized pots depending on what works for you. Also, you can choose to start with seeds or starter plants, but make sure you go for containers that are large enough to handle your plants.

Oregano

Oregano is an excellent choice for container herbs, and they help to prevent spreading, therefore, to keep your oregano under control, it is ideal for growing in containers. Oregano is very easy to grow; all you need is a small container for each plant and some potting soil. Place them in a sunny spot during the day and make sure you move them indoors during the night, especially during winter.

Spinach

To grow spinach, get an 8-inch container for each of the plants. This vegetable is a bit sensitive to heat. Therefore, you will need to protect them from direct sunlight to avoid wilting of their leaves.

Also, choose shady spots for the containers during the summer because, at this time, containers tend to get warmer. However, they grow well during the winter, and they can be successfully grown indoors. Provide them with a lot of water, so they do not dry out due to indoor heat.

Cucumbers

These plants can be quickly grown in containers. You can grow them vertically to create more space by just allowing them to vine up the side of your house, deck railings, etc. There are different varieties of cucumber, but the midget pickets, space-masters, and bush hybrids will do well in containers. Nevertheless, all cucumber varieties can be successfully grown in pots if they are adequately cared for. Make sure you create a lot of space for the growth of vines and harvest more often once they begin to produce fruits, so the vines are not weighed down and weakened.

Pineapple

You don't have to live in the tropical zones to enjoy your pineapple all year round. They can be grown in a container, and all you need to do is get a fresh pineapple and cut off the crown with part of the fruit left at the top. Soak the head in water for about one day, such that it soaks up moisture and get a gallon-size container to grow them in. Select a warm and sunny spot for your pineapple to thrive. They can be placed on the decks or balconies and be sure to always move them indoors during the night, especially during the winter.

Chives

This plant will also thrive in containers and give additional flavor to your soups, dips including baked potatoes. Chives are perennials, so they are available for planting year after year. They require some sunlight throughout the day, so always keep them close to the window, especially during the winter.

Thyme

Thyme is a useful herb for containers, and they can be grown both indoors and outdoors. You can have your herb garden in containers by planting your thyme along with the oregano, basil, and other herbs. You can as well choose to have your thyme grown alone. Clay pots are the best choice for Thyme to protect them from drying out. When growing thyme, select a container that has a good drainage hole at the bottom because they need to be well watered for them to flourish. They can also be grown indoors during winter, and they need some bits of sunlight as well during the summer and spring months.

Kale

Unlike other plants, Kale does not need much space. You can grow as much as five kale plants in a twenty-inch pot, and you will be able to move them inside during the winter season. You can start your kale container gardening with direct seeds or transplants, make sure they don't dry out. Avoid overwatering and provide them with a bit of "indirect" sunlight every day.

Peppers

You can also grow peppers in containers. Choosing the right size of the container is very important because you want to avoid your crop from getting squashed. Therefore, they need enough space to grow. Small size peppers require at least two-gallon containers while larger sizes need about five to ten-gallon pot. Ensure you expose peppers to at least eight hours of sunlight every day, so select a spot with access to adequate direct sunlight. You are free to get them back in at night but always remember to get them outdoors every morning to receive direct sunlight.

Parsley

Parsley is one of the herbs that do well in containers, and you can grow them on your balconies or porch. They don't need direct sunlight.

The partial sun is good enough for them. So growing them in small spaces or apartments will cause no harm. Avoid over-watering them, though the soil must always be kept moist. The fact that they thrive more efficiently between temperatures 40 to 80 degrees F makes them perfect for winter gardening. Protect them from too much cold by always bringing them indoors at night.

Quinoa

Quinoa is a whole grain that is very rich in nutrients, and it can easily be grown in containers. Quinoas are hardy plants, and of low maintenance, this makes them an excellent choice for container gardening. They can be grown indoors and on patios. You can cultivate them by picking up the seed and plant it directly into the potting soil in preferably large containers. However, note that these plants in pots will only get to about two feet tall, so they don't demand much space and harvesting can start by the fall.

Zucchini and Summer squash

Generally, all varieties of squash will grow well in containers, especially the summer squash. Squash is a hardy plant, and it will thrive anywhere they are being raised. Plant the seeds and pick them regularly as soon as they start growing to avoid the plants from bogging down. At initial growth, you can get three squash harvested every week and ensure you allow for new growth with a regular harvest.

Rosemary

Rosemary happens to be one of the many herbs that can be grown in a container. Opt for potting soil with a minimum amount of peat moss. Also, ensure to have some sand below the pot to help with drainage, and the soil surface can be allowed to dry out a bit in between watering. Nevertheless, don't allow them to dry out completely.

Lettuce

Lettuce is one of the most natural plants to grow in containers. The pot can be placed on the balconies or decks for adequate exposure to sunlight. Sow the lettuce seeds into the potting soil placed in a large container directly. They can also be planted alongside other greens such as the arugula if you need to manage space. Nevertheless, once the plants begin to grow, you may need to transplant them into bigger containers. But at the initial stage, you are advised to use small containers for smooth movement from the indoors to outside for adequate sunlight.

Sage

Sage is another excellent herb grown well in containers. They need adequate exposure to sunlight. Therefore, during winter, you may need to provide them with artificial lighting. When planted, position them in areas where with access to direct sunlight. The fact that they need sunlight does not mean they can't be grown indoors, make sure you give them enough sunlight during the day.

Collard greens

The collard greens need direct sunlight of least 6 hours in the spring and fall, so make sure they are exposed to the sun during the day. In the summertime, always move them to a shady spot every day. They will thrive in any season and to compensate for the sun in the winter. You might need to make use of artificial lighting for this set of plants.

Radishes

Radishes are perfect for salads recipes and can be grown in any container. They are an ideal choice of vegetable for the newbie to gardening as they are easy to grow and harvest. Ensure watering them every few days and make sure you get them exposed to sunlight every few hours a day.

Bananas

You don't have to live in tropics to grow bananas as they can be planted indoors, especially during the winter. The dwarf breeds will thrive indoors, and they are classed as perennial crops. So you will always have them available all year-round. Use a fairly deep container with drainage holes when growing your bananas to avoid drowning out your plant. During the summer, they can be placed in the balconies and decks, and you can also grow them indoors all through winter.

Watermelon

Watermelon can be grown both indoors or outdoors. Allow their vines to grow up the rails or trellises, and this will give them more space to produce more fruits. They are straightforward to grow in containers and will grow well during the winter months when placed indoors. Watermelon requires a lot of water. Thus you will need a self-watering container to cultivate them. They also demand sunlight which can be artificial, direct or partial sunlight through the window in case you have a big one.

Cauliflower

Cauliflower is another good crop for containers. The vegetable is one of the easy to grow plants, but do not grow different types in one container. For better growth, choose container per crop. You are advised to select a container that is at least eight inches deep and about eighteen inches wide for the flower to grow better. They also require direct sunlight every day and adequate drainage.

Sugar Snap Peas

Snap peas are very delicious in a stir fry and can be easily grown in containers. Therefore, you can always lay your hand on fresh sugar snap peas without having to buy them, especially when it's not the boom season. Make use of porch rail or trellis as the plants start to grow. And they will do better outdoors than indoors so you can have them placed in your balcony or on a patio during the summer or spring to achieve better results.

CHAPTER FIVE

Growing Edibles

The ability to grow most of our crops in containers provides enough opportunities. In some cases, edibles that don't grow well in the soil can be grown in containers. And you can quickly move frost plants under a cover to protect them from cold. In this chapter, I will be talking about some of the numerous edibles that can be grown in containers.

Tomatoes

Tomatoes can be grown in tubs and pots, thereby giving you easy access to one of the most common edibles in our different home recipes. They usually demand lots of nutrients with consistent watering and sunlight to get them well ripened. You can grow all the varieties of tomatoes inside containers. Nevertheless, the smaller tumbling and stockier bush varieties will not require pruning as they begin to grow.

You can plant a few marigolds along with tomatoes to add up the color and also to produce a scent that helps deter aphids. Make use of potting mix made up of some loam to help retain moisture for a longer time.

Strawberries

Strawberries are another variety of popular edibles that can be grown in containers. You can also grow them in hanging baskets, guttering, or planters that are designed for growing strawberries. The fruit also needs a lot of nutrients like tomatoes. Plant strawberry with a potting soil that can keep moisture for a longer time so that they can thrive. For the best result, mix some organic fertilizer into your potting soil before planting the fruits.

Strawberries grown with containers are usually saved from most slugs. Though you might still need to protect them from the birds, especially when they are in developing stages, you can use nets to cover and protect them from birds. The use of a mulch of straw or gravel comes handy here to help keep the fruits clean and fresh.

Carrots

The smaller varieties of carrot can be crunched raw as part of a salad recipe or having the light steamed to help preserve their taste. Carrots flourish in tall containers because it protects them against carrot-fly attack. The vegetable can be planted all through the spring and summer by starting the season with a harder variety of it. Get the tiny seeds mixed with sand to help in spacing them out as you sow, though some thinning seedlings might come in very handy. They should be harvested in stages by going for the bigger ones first so that, the smaller ones can continue growing.

Salad leaves

Salad leaves are a fast-growing vegetable, and the process of cultivating them is very straightforward, since they are shallow-rooted, making them perfect in containers. In some cases, you can harvest the whole plant at a time or pick the leave periodically, depending on how much you need.

For you to extend the harvest, it is recommended to sow a new pot of salad leaves every 3 to 4 weeks.

Make sure you protect the plants with row covers or by moving the containers into a cold frame to help in prolonging harvests. You can sow a combination of leaves - considering their leaf shapes, textures, and colors - such as the lettuce, mizuna, arugula, as well as mustard.

Swiss chard

Swiss chard is a leafy vegetable with a long harvesting period, which is why it requires a lot of space for growth. It comes in a range of different stem colors that also appears to glow with light. They can be sowed directly inside containers from spring, or you can start them in plug trays as seedlings. Make sure the plants are at least six inches apart. Swiss chard is ready to harvest about three months after sowing them. Make sure they are well fed and watered when the weather is dry.

Caring for your Edible Container

- Keep in mind that crops grown in containers do not possess very extensive roots. Therefore, the plants will need to be kept hydrated in dry weather by making sure they are watered at least two times a day during the summer.
- During the growing season, ensure getting the plants nourished with the use of liquid fertilizer.
- Make use of general-purpose feed such as the liquid seaweed for most potted crops.
- For the strawberries and tomatoes, the use of the tomato feed that have a high

concentration of potassium will come in handy.

- Most of the edibles require direct sunlight, but in the case of the Swiss chard and leafy salads, partial sunlight might be good enough, especially in hot conditions.

CHAPTER SIX

Companion Planting

The idea of companion planting has been providing excellent results to the container farmers. It involves the planting combinations of specific plants for the mutual benefits of the plants involved. The concept here is that individual plants do help each other in taking up nutrients and helping with the management of pests, while also attracting pollinators. Nevertheless, researches are still on the way to find out more planting combination that works fine. There are a few that are listed here that have been scientifically proven and will also work fine in your container garden.

Melons or squash with Flowering Herbs

All the vegetables here are known to need pollinators for production. Therefore you can plant flowering herbs such as fennel, parsley, and dill close to the squash or melon to invite insect visitors into your garden. The only way to get enough yields of these vegetables is through pollination.

Calendula with Broccoli

Calendula flowers are known to produce a sticky substance from their stems which in turn attracts aphids and gets them trapped there. Planting them next to brassica crops such as the broccoli will help to deter aphids from broccoli while also attracting beneficial ladybugs to dine on the aphids.

Radishes with Carrots

Both radishes and carrots take up nutrients from different locations in the soil, so they do not compete for nutrients or other resources. Their fast growth characterizes radishes, and they do not grow as deeply as carrots do. Carrots generally have long taproots, and it takes more time for them to mature when compared to Radishes.

Lettuce with Tomatoes or Eggplants

These plants are characterized by different growth habits which makes them beneficial to each other. Tomatoes and eggplants will generally grow taller; thereby, they are useful in shading cool-season crops like lettuce that doesn't like heat at all. Growing them with tomatoes or eggplants will also help in extending their harvest period.

Nasturtium with Cucumber

This combination involves introducing both pollinators and beneficial insects into your garden, which will, in turn, help in improving biodiversity. Nasturtiums are characterized by a unique scent that helps in repelling pests and also growing in a colorful tumble underneath.

Tomatoes with Basil or Cilantro

Apart from the belief that planting basil alongside tomatoes helps to improve the flavor of tomatoes, basil also has a strong scent that helps to prevent pests. As an added advantage, when basil or cilantro is allowed to spout flower, it will result in bringing in the pollinators.

Corn, Pole beans with Squash or Pumpkin

These combinations are popularly referred to as the three sisters. Corn gives pole beans a platform for climbing while beans will convert atmospheric oxygen into a form that can be used by both plants.

Squash and pumpkin are leaves spreading plants, thereby creating living mulch that helps in reducing weeds as well as holding of moisture.

Lettuce with Chives or Garlic

Planting of chives or garlic, which is characterized by strong smell will help in repelling aphids, thus protecting your Lettuce. *You can* also add alyssum nearby to help invite beneficial insects.

Sweet Alyssum with Swiss chard

Alyssum is an annual crop that can be quickly grown from seed between the rows of vegetables, and it is known to attract hoverflies. The Hoverflies are beneficial insects that help in the control of aphids.

Chamomile with Cabbage

Chamomile helps in inviting beneficial insects for a variety of brassicas such as cabbage. You can cut off the Chamomile and leave to get decomposed on the bed while allowing the roots to remain intact to decay and help add nutrients to the soil.

Roses with Geraniums or Chives

Generally, plants that exhibit strong smell or taste will help in deterring aphids and beetle. Though it has not been entirely proven that this works, it worth trying to prevent roses from being eaten by beetle or aphids that multiply rapidly.

CHAPTER SEVEN

Plants for Year-Round Container

During the fall, most gardeners end up disposing of, propagating or finding a home in the ground for their outdoor potted plants, which results in a waste of effort and plants themselves.

Generally, most perennials and shrubs can last several years in containers, thus help in reducing the amount of time and money spent on your pots. Depending on the kind of plant you choose, containers can provide with all-year-round food.

The growth habits of plants in containers are quite different from when grown in the ground. Containers will provide excellent drainage, but you will be the one to help supply plants with the nutrients and water they need. When it comes to shrubs and larger perennials, they are known to stay smaller in a pot depending on the plant, climate, and container type. Also, note that containers do not insulate the roots of plants from winter temperatures.

Therefore, plants that can survive all through the year have been carefully selected for you in this chapter. And not only will they survive but will also look good in terms of their quality.

Yucca and Bergenia

Yucca and bergenia are known for shining properties during the summer and fall. In the winter season when bergenia has died back, the stems that come from yellow and redtwig dogwoods help in adding to the colorful display of yucca.

While during the spring before the return of yucca and bergenia, the Lamium and pansies are known to thrive.

Yucca is highly recommended because it combines effortlessly with many plants. It is characterized by sword-like leaves which are 2-inch wide with thin and dark green margins. They also have golden-yellow centers with curly fibers along the edges with a spiky architectural shape. They grow as high as two to three feet with an equal spread. Yuccas will thrive in sunny and dry conditions, and they also tolerate shade.

During the summer, fragrant creamy-white flowers will emerge from the center of the plant on three to six-foot stems. Nevertheless, during the late winter, the foliage becomes a little flat, but it will perk up again during the spring. You are advised to pull off the old leaf to maintain a tidy appearance.

Golden Creeping Jenny

This plant is very reliable for all year round containers. It is a 4-inch tall plant that cascades beautifully over the rim of a pot. The leave is golden with a coin shape. This plant loves lots of water and as a result, will grow very well in a water garden. It also likes partial shade, though it tolerates full sun and the soil must always be moist.

Green Mountain Boxwood

The green mountain boxwood is slow-growing shrubs that maintain a dark green color all through winter. This plant is usually 5 feet tall and 3 feet wide but growing them in containers makes them even smaller. Make sure they are protected from strong winds in semi-shaded locations. You will also want to engage in the periodical rotation of the pot to balance the exposure of the plant to light while avoiding the development of bare sides.

Bergenia

This plant has bold leaves that shine well in containers. It is characterized by glossy, green, oval leaves, and it is strong providing a bold element in a pot. Bergenia has leaves with sizes of about ten to twenty inches long and are six to eight inches wide. It is recommended to have them grown under full sun or light shade.

Emerald arborvitae

This plant comes in handy where some height is needed, providing an appealing view all year round because it retains its vibrant green color during the winter. Their foliage shape and texture that makes them easy to combine with other plants. Keep in mind that growing emerald arborvitae in a container will keep them below their natural sizes of 15 feet high and four feet wide. They can be planted in full sun or light shades.

Japanese Pieris

Pieris is a deer-resistant shrub, and during the spring, they are known to have varying colors such as glossy red, salmon pink, and creamy white depending on the cultivar. During winter, the flower buds will be showy, which is usually dark red and with some opening to shades of pink. During the early spring, you will have a delicate three to six-inch-long racemes of white with urn-shaped blossoms coming up from these shrubs. Japanese

Pieris grows well in full sun and full shades. It is, however, essential to protect them from the harsh winds during winter and intense sun.

CHAPTER EIGHT

Maintenance Tips for Healthy Containers

Containers that have once been rich in color and foliage tend to fade and fail, gradually becoming worn out as the midsummer begins to roll in. As the temperatures start to rise, pretty blossoms and fleshy leaves begin to wither and disappear. Fortunately, with proper care, your containers can flourish with vibrant health all summer.

Although in these modern times, gardens and nurseries have a fantastic choice of lovely, healthy plants which makes it very easy to design an attractive looking container. Nevertheless, it is more important to keep them vibrant and maintain their healthy state from spring all through autumn.

The following is a brief review of the crucial steps that can be taken to create and maintain a brilliant display all through summer:

- The first step towards having a healthy container is selecting the correct size of the pot, which is determined by different factors. Choosing a small planter with crowded roots will result in less water, oxygen, and nutrients available to the roots and all these are important for their healthy growth.
- On the other hand, when containers are too big, they will result in having excess moisture in the soil, thereby cutting off oxygen and eventually drowning the roots. Also, planters

that have too much space with moist soil will help in solving most plant problems.

- In a situation where the recommended spacing is ten to twelve inches, for example, you will make sure the plants are about six to eight inches apart. Generally, if their average growth is about ten to 12 inches tall, you should opt for a pot that is nearly half the size or width of around six to eight inches. In the case of plants that grow between 24 to 36 inches tall, you will need a larger container of about 24 inches in diameter. Also, ensure your pot is composed of drainage holes with the required material below it to enable excess water are flowing out smoothly.

- It is also advisable to invert a smaller plastic pot over the drainage holes if adding more weight is an issue. There has also been some controversy as regards styrene from Styrofoam leeching into edibles. It was concluded that the low levels of styrene that are found in packaged food are due to the leaching that comes from the polystyrene containers in which they were packed. It is therefore recommended to make use of gravel, pieces of broken pottery, pebbles, nutshells, sticks, pinecones, or coffees as your drainage.

- Also, note that container plants don't like their roots sitting in water. It will result in a wet root environment that will cause most bedding plants to sulk and have low growth. They can also cause the roots to rot, which makes planters inconvenient.

- Drainage is also required to help provide your potted roots with adequate aeration. Because without this, and it will be hard for them to breathe and get easy access to oxygen.

CHAPTER NINE

Vertical Gardening

In situations where you have only a small outdoor space available, you will want to practice vertical gardening. Just fill up space with colorful flowers, herbs, and vines. Vertical gardening has so many advantages which the most significant being the fact that they end up saving you a lot of space, especially the floor spaces. Here are the simple tips for you to expertly carry out your vertical gardening:

Decide on the Garden Type

There are different types of vertical gardens that you can engage in. However, the easiest of them all is the container-style garden that allows potted plants to get attached to a wall or gives the opportunity of having them displayed in rows. The pocket garden is another type in which plants are tucked into pockets that are made from canvas or felt.

Generally, vertical garden can be grown in a big plastic or wooden fence planter with panels or slots. For wooden pallets, they possess landscaping fabric stapled at the bottom and the sides of the pallet while the inside is filled with soil with the plants grown in the slat openings.

Consider the Placement

Vertical gardening can be placed anywhere from the outdoors to indoors. When determining where to place your garden, you will need to consider the type of sun exposure your plants need. For instance, if you plan to plant succulents, it is advisable to choose a space that has half exposure in contrast to the full sun or full shade. You can hang your containers outside in summer and bring them back indoors in the winter.

Selecting your Pants

Apart from the succulents for your vertical garden, you can also grow herbs, native perennials, vegetables, ferns because of their r flexibility. However, you can try out the herbaceous plants other than the woody plants because the former is a lot more flexible in terms of the way they fall. Herbaceous possess soft and green stems which helps them in dropping down. On the other hand, woody plants such as shrubs, vines, and trees are made up of woody stems that make them grow in a parallel pattern. And they will stick out instead of flowing down.

Combine Plants of the Same Growth Habit

Generally, you can opt for an all sun or all shade plants as well as choosing plants with the same growth rate. Except for other reasons, if you select a plant that has a slow growth rate and plants it next to one that grows faster, the more aggressive one will shade out the latter.

Consider Planting Basics

Noted that the vertical garden will dry out quickly, just like pots. It is therefore advisable to make use of the potting soil as it helps in retaining water and holds in moisture. Gravity which pulls down the water should also be taken into consideration, therefore place the ones that require more water at the bottom of your vertical garden.

Beforehand Preparation

If you choose wooden pallets or containers that have panels, it's ideal for growing plants in a horizontal pattern for some weeks. To help the roots in establishing themselves while holding the soil in place. If you are trying to cultivate it vertically first, it will results in the soil bowing to gravity and being pulled down. You are also advised to elevate the container slowly into a vertical position as the week progresses.

Drip Irrigation System

At the initial stage, a vertical garden does require more maintenance than the traditional in-ground gardening. Noted that the living walls are more compact, resulting in them possessing less soil, which is why you will need to get them watered often. In a situation where the living wall is big, you might need to integrate the drip irrigation. Drip system involves the use of hoses and timers to help regulate which holes at the bottom of the planters allow for water to drip down. You can make use of the regular watering as well but make sure that water is equally distributed.

Consider Having Extra Plants

It is usual for some greens to die out in vertical gardening. You will lose some plants, thereby creating some holes which will make your garden look ugly. These extras will come in handy as a backup plan so that you can easily have them plugged into the new one. It's especially useful if you are practicing a container-style garden where the plants have more separation between them.

CHAPTER TEN

Managing Pests and Plant Diseases

There are different natural and organic ways of dealing with pest and disease issues in the garden, most of which have proved useful over recent years. In modern times, most of these techniques are usually referred to as Integrated Pest Management (IPM). They can also be referred to as Organic Pest Management (OPM).

For effective pest and plant disease management, close observation of your garden more often is the fundamental way to start. The ability to recognize in time that your plant is stressed will allow you to take proactive steps to help keep these pests and plant diseases in check. Nevertheless, leaving these pests and diseases unchecked will only result in an unhealthy garden with an unhealthy environment.

To help discourage these garden pests and diseases from causing damage to your garden, without having to use synthetic, non-organic controls, you are advised to consider the following techniques.

- Make sure you choose the best site and soil for the type of plants you are growing. And it will go a long way in reducing plant stress and its vulnerability to diseases and pests. If you expose your plants to excessive or too little sun, shade, fertilizer, or water, they can be stressed up. You are advised to make use of aged compost to help provide your plants with all the nutrients they need.

- You are advised to choose plant species or varieties that are resistant. Make sure you check your seed packets including the plant labels for the pest and diseases as well as resistance. Always try to mix different plant families to create diversity. This is effective in preventing the rapid spread of pests and plant diseases that are known for attacking specific plant groups.
- Engage in pruning or pinching to help in removing damaged or diseased leaves with branches. And it will also help in increasing the light as well as air circulation in your garden.
- You can and-pick insect pests off the plants in your container garden. You can get insects such as snails, slugs, large adult insects,

caterpillars. You can easily handpick and drop them off into soapy water.

- Make use of lures to get insects trapped using both olfactory and visual. For instance, making use of yellow sticky boards can help control whiteflies, cucumber beetles, thrips, and cabbage worms.
- You can make use of pest barricade such as a sticky bands or floating row covers to get the pests off the plants and planting beds.
- Invite beneficial insects to your container garden. Examples of these beneficial insects include lacewings, lady beetles, spined soldier beetles, etc. You can also grow plants that will provide nectar and pollen for beneficial insects.

- Always keep your container garden free from plant debris. Remember that pest insects are capable of hiding or finding shelter in dropped or dead leaves. Get the soil turned during the fall or in between plantings to help expose these hidden pests.

- Bacteria, viruses, or fungi can be engaged to help kill some of these pests and garden diseases. Bacillus thuringiensis is commonly used, and it is a bacteria species that gives out toxins that are poisonous to most insect pests.

- Finally, some pests and plant diseases can be controlled with the use of non-toxic sprays such as a forceful spray of water with the garden hose to effectively dislodge them.

CHAPTER ELEVEN

Harvesting and Storing the Bounty

The spring season is the perfect period to start preserving some of the fresh produce that you must have grown in your container garden. An essential part of your garden plan should be what to do with the fresh produce that comes from your garden. There are different ways of using your fresh produce which includes making fresh salads, sandwiches, and crudités for meals as well as snacks.

Nevertheless, when you have too much fresh produce, and you need to preserve some. That is if you have run of options of giving it to your family and friends or selling it off in some farmers' market.

Some crops are suitable to be used immediately they are harvested. However, you can preserve some, either by freezing, canning, or drying them for meals in the cold times.

Freezing your fresh produce is an excellent way of preserving them as long as you have freezer space available. For freezing purposes, you will need plastic freezer containers or freezer quality bags to be used when your fresh crop is ready for freezing.

Canning is very advantageous when it comes to preserving fresh produce, in the sense that you can store them in jars without having to take up extra freezer space. Once they are canned, find a cool, dry place to get them preserved. Some of the storing equipment that can be used includes, lids, a jar lifter, rings, water bath canner, or pressure canner.

And they depend on the type of crop you are preserving.

Another way of preserving your bounty is by getting them dehydrated in a situation where you don't have ample storage space available. You can dehydrate by making use of a dehydrator or oven. However, you can select a dehydrator that contains a thermostat that will allow you to choose between different numerical temperatures, instead of going for the traditional low, medium, or high.

CONCLUSION

The ability to have your food grown under your nose becomes very important. That is why container gardening is a practice for all, and the good news is that anyone can do this, no matter how new you are to the term "gardening."

Every tips and instruction highlighted in this book are essential for gardeners and even beginners that are planning to venture into container gardening. If you understand the well-being of container plants, their requirements, and how to respond to their challenges, you will be able to provide them with the perfect conditions to thrive. Also, anyone planning to begin gardening in containers ought to learn about the conditions of the seeds first to help them break out of the dormancy and germinate successfully.

I hope that after reading this book, you must have been well equipped with the needed knowledge for your container garden to flourish. And I hope this book has sparked your curiosity into having a deeper appreciation for the miracles taking place in your garden and the environment around you.

Welcome to the world of CONTAINER GARDENING! Enjoy!

Manufactured by Amazon.ca
Bolton, ON